Now That I'm ~~Middle-Aged~~ Mature

I Know What I Want To Be
When I Grow Up

Sylvia Morice

ISBN-13: **978-0-9880509-2-1**

Also by Sylvia Morice

Postcards From Home
Needs
Short Journeys
A Small Steel Box
Going Home and Other Stories
I Dream In Color

DEDICATION

To Faye and Les for encouraging me to keep writing and for 'getting' my slightly-warped humor.

CONTENTS

Author's Note   i

1   Now That I'm Mature   Pg 1

2   Jigsaw Puzzle Addictions   Pg 5

3   Who's Afraid of the Big Bad Wolf?   Pg 11

4   There's A Mouse In My House   Pg 15

5   Organization Is Not My Forte   Pg 23

6   Old Dog, New Tricks   Pg 27

7   I Have Met the Enemy, and She is Mosquito   Pg 32

8   Oh Where, Oh Where, Did My Little Pendent Go?   Pg 38

9   Up, Up and Away   Pg 45

10   What I Had NOT Planned to Do On My Vacation   Pg 52

11   Random Friday Thoughts   Pg 61

12   Cruising to Hawaii   Pg 65

13   Hi Ho, Hawaii   Pg 68

14   Losing My Snorkeling Virginity   Pg 72

15   Playing Ukulele on the High Seas   Pg 77

16   Aloha Hawaii, Hello Ice and Snow   Pg 85

17   No More Bucket Lists   Pg 88

About the Author   Pg 97

AUTHOR'S NOTE

The stories in this collection first saw life as stand-alone blog posts or periodical articles. Thanks to all who commented that they enjoyed my work and laughed or giggled or guffawed at my sense of humor. Your encouragement inspired me to combine the posts into this collection. Hope you enjoy them!.

Now That I'm Mature

I have great news to share with you—I've finally decided what to do with the rest of my life now that I'm mature.

Whew! What a load off my mind.

Never mind the fact that I'm in the high-end of middle-age already and you think I should have matured years ago; one thing you learn when you're finally mature is that maturity has nothing to do with age.

But now I will do the 'dance of joy' because, "Hi-Diddle-Dee-Dee, a humorist I'll be.

That's right, I've decided to become a humorist.

I imagine I'll be pretty good at it, too, and I'm really looking forward to spending the rest of my life humoring people.

But I read somewhere that it's important for humorists to target specific groups with their special wit, so before I concentrate on writing ever-so-humorous material, I guess that I need to decide exactly whom it is I will humor.

I've really put a lot of thought into this and at first I decided that I should cater to children, but when I tried my material out on them, I discovered that I really don't understand the little tykes.

I know that they're cute, but their minds can't seem to grasp my sophisticated humor.

For example, they belly laugh if they see me trip and fall on my walk to the front of the room, but when I try to tell them a really funny story, such as the one about the train that ran over my father's dog, Jed, they become upset.

Before I ever got anywhere near the punch line they interrupted me.

"Did Jed die?" they asked, eyes like Frisbees.

"Yes, yes, but you see, the train that ran over him..." Well, I couldn't continue; the children's sobs drowned my voice, and two dramatic little girls actually ran from the room, calling for their mommies.

So I guess I won't write humor for children; I like them too much to make them so miserable.

What about seniors then? Maybe they've lived long enough to develop the finely tuned sense of humor needed to appreciate me.

My grandmother lived to be ninety and she used to laugh at me sometimes.

"Poor Sylvia," she'd say, her grandmotherly voice a mixture of love and pity, "We can only hope that she marries well."

Hmm--perhaps seniors have lived *too* long to appreciate me; I may need to rethink my strategy.

I have made progress, though.

By ruling out the **very-young** and the **very-old**, I've narrowed the field down to the **in-between**.

That would be you.

I haven't inflicted my humor on an audience of in-betweeners yet, but I'm pretty sure I'll be a rousing success when I do.

If I'm not, it will simply mean that even in-betweeners are too young or too old to enjoy me, and I'll simply have to target another group.

Maybe I'll have to focus on the *not-yet-born* or the *long-since dead.*

I won't give up until I find my audience; I know that.

Another news item I read recently said that in order to put an audience at ease, humorists should talk about themselves, so I think I'll give that a try, too.

Now I realize that you've lived your life up to now without knowing anything about me at all, and I realize you're probably content to maintain the status quo, but I'll forge ahead anyway and then you can decide whether you were more contented before or after I talk.

I could tell you that I'm tall, slim, blond and have perfect teeth, but I'd really like you to think of me as a humorist, not just a common liar. I'm sure there must be a world of difference between the two, although I wouldn't want to swear to it.

Oops—I just remembered that I don't like talking about myself. Besides, by now you probably have a pretty good idea as to what I don't look like, and I'm pretty certain that I know what you don't look like, so this leaves us on an even footing.

If I'm rambling and you think I should stop, please just say so. Remember, though, that humorists sometimes ramble for three or four pages before ever saying anything remotely humorous. Then again, humorists sometimes ramble for three or four pages and NEVER say anything humorous. Sort of an unpredictable group, aren't we?

But I suppose that it is time now for me to be humorous. Just give me a moment while I think of a subject.

Something humorous. Something humorous. No, no, don't help me. There must be something amusing I can share with you.

What about politics? Nope, nothing funny there. Religion? No, I promised my mother I wouldn't joke about religion. Sex? Nothing funny about that at my age.

Something funny... Well, I could talk about the dream I had last night.

In my dream I was a taxi driver and Shirley MacLaine was my passenger. At the corner of Maple and Sycamore, Shirley had some sort of vision about me and she informed me that I wasn't really a taxi driver at all; I was actually a reincarnation of someone important with the initials S.L.

Shirley said that I was either a Stanley Lincock, or a Stephen Leacock, or Shirley's friend's great-great uncle Samuel Lamrock. Shirley wasn't sure which S.L. I was, but she was certain I was one of them.

I really don't think that Shirley would make this stuff up, so I choose to believe her.

And if I could have my pick of the three possibilities she mentioned in my dream, I'd like to think that I'm Samuel Lamrock, because according to the stories Shirley told me about him Sammy always knew when to put a lamp shade on his head.

Now that's humorous.

My Jigsaw Puzzle Addiction

I just completed a 1000 piece jigsaw puzzle.

It's a picture of penguins—lots and lots and lots of penguins, in shades of blue and gray and white and yellow—many, many shades of blue and gray and white and yellow.

It was a difficult puzzle to put together, or at least to put together without the help of a sharp knife to make the pieces fit. Each piece was a challenge and was studied and rotated and occasionally cursed.

Occasionally, even the maker of the puzzle was cursed, and the givers of the puzzle (my children) were cursed. Come to think of it, there was a fair amount of cursing going on whenever I sat down to work on that puzzle.

I hate that puzzle.

But hating a puzzle is the least of my problems. My big problem is that I am a jigsaw puzzle addict.

As soon as I open the cardboard box and begin the hunt for the pieces that will form the puzzle frame, my obsession takes over.

I lose track of time.

I forget about meals and about drinking my eight glasses of water a day. I forget to go to bed at night, even though my back and neck scream from being hunched over a table for hours on end. I forget to call my friends and family, forget to read the daily paper, and forget to limit myself to a reasonable amount of time each day to devote to this hobby.

I am a sad, sad case.

A couple of years ago on Christmas morning I received several new puzzles, including the penguin one I just completed.

I also received another 1000 piece puzzle, an idyllic lake scene, complete with a canoe, a dog, two men fishing from the canoe, and a beautiful summer home on an island in the background, with trees for shade and flags waving in the light summer breeze.

I hate that puzzle already and I haven't even opened the package yet.

I also received a 768 piece puzzle that my children were thoughtful enough to order for me online using one of my own pictures as the image (which, by the way, they pilfered from where it was stored, ever so nicely, inside my computer).

The photo is a shot of a marsh near where I live, and I remember taking that picture late one fall day, thinking that the scene looked so tranquil.

The picture turned out great—the sky is blue and white—many, many shades of blue and white, and the marsh grass and bales of hay are brown—many, many shades of brown. That's all the picture consists of—sky and marsh and bales of hay.

Now I hate that picture, almost as much as I hate the puzzle that it became.

My sadistic children also gave me a tiny puzzle—only four inches high by six inches wide. How difficult could that be to put together?

I thought for sure I would be able to complete it, start to finish, in under an hour.

I was wrong.

The first inkling I had that I was mistaken was when I saw that the puzzle came not only with 234 tiny pieces but also with its own little pink set of teeny-tiny tweezers.

What an odd accessory to accompany a puzzle, I thought, before I opened the box and stared at the miniscule jigsaw parts.

Ah, now the tweezers make sense.

That tiny puzzle now sits on my dining room table, complete except for three wayward pieces that won't fit into the puzzle, no matter how many times I twist them and turn them and try to squish them into place.

I am stumped.

Did I mention that I hate that puzzle.

And then, just when I thought there could be nothing worse than a 234-piece tiny puzzle, I spied one more puzzle gift peeking out of my Christmas stocking. Surely this would be an ordinary puzzle, simple enough for a young child to complete.

Silly me, for thinking such a thing.

This 9-piece puzzle had a warning on the box: "Over 300,000 wrong ways to assemble the pieces, but only ONE right way!"

Isn't that just great?

I spent many, many hours that day and evening trying many, many, many combinations of those 9 stupid puzzle pieces until I finally found the correct one.

Could I do it again? I doubt it. Will I try it again?

Not sure, but I am sure that I hate that puzzle.

***

Last summer I spent a couple of weeks visiting my brother and sister-in-law in Alberta, and my sister-in-law, being the sweetheart that she is, purchased a 1000-piece jigsaw puzzle for me to work on, "if I became bored," she said.

The box sat on the dining table for a couple of days before I cracked.

I HAD to start the puzzle, right then. I am not superhuman—I can only withstand temptation for so long before I cave in.

That puzzle depicted a peaceful forest scene; it had trees and bushes and forest flowers and a fuzzy fawn lying near some decomposing vegetation (old logs). It was a picturesque blend of greens and browns and grays and pinks—many, many shades of greens and browns and grays and pinks.

Needless to say I spent a copious number of hours bent over that puzzle, pawing through the assorted pieces, before I finally put the last piece into place.

I hate that puzzle.

But I am going to reform. I have decided that I will wait a full week before I start another puzzle, and when I do begin the next one, I'll only work on it for an hour or so at a time. I'll remember to eat and to drink my eight glasses of water a day. I will not let my obsession take over my life again.

I promise.

Okay, now that I've made that promise I feel that I'm back in control of my life. And in fact, I'm feeling so good about it that I'm sure I could actually start a new puzzle today, right now, secure in the knowledge that I will not obsess over this puzzle the way I did with previous ones.

Yes, this is definitely a good feeling, being in control.

Now the only decision that remains for me to make is which puzzle to open. So many choices, so many puzzle pieces.

Hmm... I think I'll tackle the 768-piece puzzle of the sky and the marsh and the bales of hay.

And I'll just work on it for an hour or so.

I promise.

***

Update

I simply had to let you know my good news--I just completed the 768-piece puzzle of the Tantramar Marsh that my children gave me for Christmas; I knew you'd want to know.

I also tore apart the 4 inch by 6 inch Santa's Woodland puzzle (remember those three remaining pieces that refused to fit anywhere?), and I finally figured out how to put it together correctly.

But the bad news is I haven't kicked my jigsaw puzzle addiction.

Remember when I said that I would limit my puzzle-work to an hour or two a day--that didn't pan out at all. No matter how many times I tried to stand up and walk away from the puzzle, my butt remained glued to the chair for hours at a time.

What can I say? I am a weak person.

Recently I mentioned my weakness to my daughter during a telephone chat.

"Why do you think that's a weakness?" she said. "Working on jigsaw puzzles is a hobby you enjoy, and yes, you may become a bit preoccupied when you're in the middle of a puzzle and you work at it for long stretches at a time without taking a break, but what's the harm in that, other than possibly getting a backache?"

Now, I know that my daughter is a very smart daughter and I do love her, so I've decided that I'm going to listen to her.

Tonight I'm going to slip a movie into the DVD player, switch on my powerful floor lamp, and open a new puzzle box. I'm going to work on this puzzle for as long as I like, too, or at least until my back starts complaining.

I've realized that as far as addictions go, this one is relatively harmless.

And I do so love the smell of new cardboard.

WHO'S AFRAID OF THE BIG BAD WOLF?

The other day, when I was driving to my cottage to help close it for the winter, I had a half-hour of quiet time to myself to think.

I do this a lot when I'm driving somewhere–I rarely bother listening to the radio or a compact disc; I'm happy just to think my thoughts and see where they take me.

The other day my thoughts took me to 'fears'. What am I still afraid of that I've been afraid of since I was a little girl, and what fears have I overcome or outgrown or reasoned away over the years?

I immediately thought of a couple of fears I've had since my childhood, and that I imagine I'll carry with me to my grave.

One of my fears is of the dentist.

Now, I know there is absolutely no good reason to fear a dentist this day and age but it is very difficult to erase childhood phobias, and when I was little I had a very good reason for fearing our local tooth-extractor.

My family was fairly poor and with four children to feed, clothe, and send to school there wasn't money left over to schedule regular dental appointments.

I only went to see our local dentist (who is long gone now), when I had a toothache and something needed to be filled or pulled, or the one time that I hit my mouth on a table and a nerve in one of my front teeth had to be removed because it was dying.

I don't ever remember going to the dentist as a child to have my teeth cleaned; that luxury was reserved for children whose families had money left over at the end of a month.

So my trips to the dentist were traumatic: I was afraid of the smells and of the sounds and of the needles, and I was even afraid of the dentist himself.

Our dentist was a hunched-over, skinny man with thinning hair and a receding hairline, and even though he spoke calmly and moved about the room quietly, I could never warm up to him. I think perhaps it's difficult to warm up to someone who is in the business of causing you pain, or at least that's how I felt.

I especially didn't like looking into his eyes when his face was only a few inches away from mine. His eyes were icy blue, like regular blue eyes except maybe bleached in the sun, and they were cold and empty-looking, as if the dentist had already died and someone just forgot to bury him.

I have no idea what my dentist was like outside the office; perhaps he was a wonderful man and an all-around amazing human being, but I only knew him as someone who took very large needles (the size of a turkey baster), and jammed them into my cheeks or gums or roof of my very tender mouth.

And once he stuck his turkey-baster needle into me he didn't just hold it steady while the freezing agent took effect; no, he wiggled it around and around, just to be sure I received as much stinging and stabbing pain as possible.

I've never recovered from my fear of having needles poked into my mouth.

Even with today's modern dentistry, where the needles are minuscule compared to my childhood dentist's torture devices, I cringe when I see one heading in my direction.

I'm actually a big baby when I'm in the dentist chair, and that's a sad way to go through life.

***

When my husband and I had children we knew that we wanted them to have regular dental checkups beginning as soon as they had enough teeth in their tiny little mouths for the dentist to see. So I took them every six months, and they received brightly colored toothbrushes, stickers of big smiling teeth and happy little children dancing around a container of floss, and positive feedback from the hygienist, the dentist, and us. They never minded their twice-a-year trips to the dentist because they saw them as part of a routine.

I used to sit in the waiting room and read magazines while my children had their teeth cleaned, and while they swished fluoride around their mouths, and when they had ex-rays taken to make sure their teeth were growing in properly and there were no cavities lurking beneath the gum surface.

And I started going to the dentist regularly, too.

After all, how can any good mother spout, "Do as I say, not as I do," and expect her children to follow blindly? So I began having regular checkups and cleanings, and even had a few old fillings replaced.

Now, when the hygienist comes out of her office and calls my name I bravely follow her to the inner sanctum and crawl onto the reclining lounge chair, then lie back with my feet crossed and my arms folded over my chest.

If I look as if I'm waiting for the grim reaper to arrive and cart my body away to the local undertaker it's because that is exactly how I feel lying there.

As the nice hygienist does her best (I don't think I've ever had a male hygienist), to put me at ease with small talk and a soothing voice, I try my hardest not to hyperventilate or pass out.

The dentist I have currently is very nice, too; he is gentle when he uses his instruments of torture to pick and probe at my teeth and gums, and his eyes still show a reflection of a soul somewhere behind the irises, so that helps to ease my anxiety a little bit.

But I still can't seem to get over my fear of going to the dentist, and in all likelihood I will probably always fear going. That is just me and one of my pitiful phobias rearing its ugly head.

Speaking of fears and phobias, do you want to know how I feel about mice? You do?

Well, I'm afraid of them, too, and think I'll write about that phobia next.

Until then, Happy Brushing and Flossing

THERE'S A MOUSE IN MY HOUSE

Recently I wrote a post about a childhood phobia of mine that has carried through to adulthood—the fear of going to the dentist, and I received quite a few comments from fellow bloggers and readers about it.

Apparently this fear is not unique to my spineless self but is experienced throughout the adult population, especially throughout the adult population of those aged fifty and over.

So now I do not feel so alone in this phobia, and for that I am thankful.

But what about this next fear on my list?

I am afraid of mice (and of course of rats, which should go without saying).

I imagine this fear began when I was a child growing up in an old farmhouse; I used to hear the squeaks and scurrying of mice conversing overhead, and I'd hear the thumping of rats running around in their army boots in the wall beside the head of my bed as I tried to go to sleep at night in the dark.

Hearing those sounds above and around me certainly made falling asleep difficult and made dreaming of sugarplum fairies next-to-impossible, and more than once I headed to my parents' bedroom to complain about the four-legged races taking place in my ceiling and walls.

But mice and rats were a fact of life for people living in an old home in the country.

Sure, we had cats in the barn, and they looked after the mice and rats that ventured anywhere near that territory, but they did little to discourage the critters that took refuge in our farmhouse every fall and winter.

I figure there were just too many of them for the cats to handle, and the mice knew lots of secret tunnels and hiding places that the kitties couldn't find.

So the humans and the rodents co-existed, sort-of peacefully, except for when I had to go to the cellar.

I can't say that I ever actually SAW a mouse or a rat in the dirt-floor cellar of our farmhouse, but every time I was sent down there to fetch potatoes or carrots from the cold room, or pickles or beets or green tomato chow from the storage shelves, I was sure that I would come face-to-face with just such a dreaded creature.

So I only went down to the cellar against my will.

Every time that my mother told me to go down the stone steps to the grey cellar door and unlatch it and push it open and turn on the overhead light and find my way to the cold room or storage shelves, I protested.

But my protests did no good whatsoever.

Mom knew all the tricks of the trade–I was the third child out of four and most tricks had already been tried by my older sister and brother, so I was stuck with having to obey her.

I carried out my missions as if on a stop-watch–I practically sprinted through the old wooden door, down the dark cellar hallway past the wood furnaces and up the little incline to the wooden shelving unit where mom stored the preserves, and then I'd see if I could set a new record running back to the entrance and slamming the door behind me as I finally took a breath of air.

I ran as if my life depended on it, because I truly thought it did.

I thought that it would only be a matter of time before a gang of rats or mice who 'owned' the cellar territory would capture and torture me as punishment for wandering into their turf.

Once I grew up, got married and moved into my own place I pretty much forgot about my mouse phobia--until my husband and I transferred to St. John's, Newfoundland in 1998.

We loved St. John's; it is a beautiful city in Canada's most easterly province and is full of character (and characters).

We bought a modern ranch-style home on a corner lot in a nice neighborhood and settled into a routine of working and entertaining and relaxing with our friends and our Miniature Schnauzer, Bobbie Jean (BJ for short).

The lot behind our home was empty, not yet developed, and we liked it that way. No neighbors staring into our kitchen, no children throwing baseballs through our windows, no cats teasing our dog.

Then one day a construction company came and began to clear the field.

Oh, oh, I thought. *I wonder what this will mean.*

Well, I found out that it meant that the little field mice, who had probably been living ever-so-peacefully behind us in the vacant lot, found themselves evicted from their home, and so of course they had to search for a new warm place to rest their heads.

What they found was a lovely modern ranch-style home on a corner lot in a nice neighborhood occupied by a woman and her husband and their Miniature Schnauzer, Bobbie Jean (BJ for short).

***

One evening Bobby Jean and I were catching up on the suppertime news, snuggled together on the sofa in the den, when out of nowhere a mouse scampered across the floor in front of us, ran behind the television stand and disappeared.

I screamed.

Bobby Jean looked at the mouse, then looked at me, then looked back at the mouse, then yawned and snuggled in tighter against me.

I was not amused.

"I thought Schnauzers were bred to hunt down rats and mice and exterminate them," I said to my snoring dog. "So, exterminate something."

BJ stirred in her sleep, perhaps chasing a rabbit or an imaginary rodent across an open field in Germany.

But as far as the mouse in my den was concerned, it was safe. Bobbie Jean had no more inclination to hop down off the sofa and corner a mouse than I had to chew off my right arm with my teeth.

When my husband arrived home from work I managed to non-hysterically (well, mostly non-hysterically), tell him about our visitor, and he said, and I quote, "Don't worry about one little mouse, dear. I'll set a trap out for it tonight and that will be the end."

It wasn't the end.

Soon we found more mice, then more mice, then more. My husband set traps for them every night and caught at least a dozen tiny little creatures whose sole crime was to invade our home and leave little mouse-gifts in our cupboards and drawers and scare me half-to-death every time one scampered across the floor in front of me.

BJ, on the other hand, was not in the least bothered or concerned by these new guests; she simply stared at them as they ran past her to disappear behind the television stand or corner desk or underneath the sofa.

Something had to change.

I declared that we either had to relocate or call in a professional to rid our home of these pests.

My hubby didn't want to move, so the next day I followed an exterminator through the house as he searched for 'evidence' of our visitors and put out traps and poisons to thwart the tiny invaders.

"Not t'all unusual," he said. "Tis cause of the building going on behind you. This will catch 'em, for sure."

Actually, I can't swear that these were the specific words he spoke; he had a very strong Newfoundland accent, and I had a difficult time interpreting what he was saying to me...but to the best of my knowledge he was a real exterminator and knew what he was talking about. Otherwise why would I have paid him $125.00?

After the traps and poisons were set all my husband and I (and BJ) could do was wait for results.

In the meantime, life carried on.

I had to invite seven women to my home on the following Wednesday at one PM. for an afternoon of bridge. (I had joined a bridge group when we moved to St.

John's and the players took turns hosting the bi-weekly event.)

That particular Wednesday was my turn, so it really wasn't my fault or my choice that these women were due to arrive at my home that fateful day, or that they quite reasonably expected it to be rodent-free.

That morning I made sure that my house was spotless.

My kitchen was *Martha Stewart* clean, the bathroom was so immaculate that royalty would have felt at home, the living room was neat and orderly, and the dining room table shone.

I had the bridge tables set up, the fancy bridge table-cloths covering the tables, and the finger foods ready for a mid-afternoon snack break.

All I had left to do was change my clothes, pour a cup of coffee to calm my nerves, and sit and wait.

I changed my clothes and walked back to the kitchen, then decided to take one last swing through the dining room and living room.

I was part way around my dining room table when I spotted it—a half-dead mouse sitting square in the middle of the beige carpet, right next to my buffet and hutch.

I screamed; the mouse fell over a bit.

I screamed again. The mouse didn't move.

What to do, what to do, what to do?

I was alone. My husband was away on business; he couldn't come home even if he wanted to, and I didn't know anybody that could arrive on a white horse to save the day.

So I phoned a friend in a neighboring province.

After I screamed my problem into the receiver, and she figured out what I was babbling about, she suggested that I grab a broom and hit the mouse with it, then push it onto a dustpan and deposit it into the trash.

I thought she had finally lost her mind.

In the end, though, I had no choice but to follow her advice—I had seven women about to arrive at my door, and I didn't know how I would explain the half-dead mouse on the floor, or how we would manage to ignore it all afternoon while trying to decide on hearts or spades or no-trump.

I found my broom and dustpan, mustered up my courage while I tried to stop screaming, and sneaked up on the mouse from behind.

I knew that the mouse appeared comatose, but I didn't want to take any chances, so I chose the surprise attack.

I screamed once more, very loudly, then swatted at the mouse with my broom and watched as it fell over on its side, as still as snow that falls on a winter morning.

Oh—by the way—it was winter—February, freezing cold and there was at least two feet of snow in my yard. But that didn't matter to me at the time.

I continued to scream while I set the dustpan down on the carpet, and while I used the broom to push the mouse onto the dustpan, and while I picked up the dustpan and carried it to my kitchen door and opened the door and ran down the snow-covered steps and across my back yard and THREW it as hard as I could over the fence that separated my property from the new building site behind me.

I think I even continued to scream all the way back up my steps and into my home.

Which now makes me think—if it had been an axe murderer/rapist/strangler in my dining room and I had screamed as loudly as I did, and still no one appeared at my door to ask if everything was okay, what does that say about today's neighbors in today's subdivisions?

I guess I was fortunate that it was just a mouse in my house.

After I calmed down from my hysterical jaunt outside, I searched the house from room to room, looking for any other signs of dead or half-dead vermin lying on my floor.

Luckily, I didn't find any and the afternoon of bridge went off without a hitch.

I do wonder, though, what the bridge gals would have said had they arrived a bit early and found an hysterical crazy woman swinging a broom and screaming at the top of her lungs.

I'm just glad I didn't find out.

After a few weeks we finally eradicated the mice from our home and resumed a more normal existence.

But I am still afraid of them (and of course of rats, which goes without saying).

Oh, and did I mention that we moved from Newfoundland the following winter, but that when I flew back to St.John's one February weekend to meet with our real estate agent and prepare for the movers to arrive, I found another half-dead mouse in the middle of my kitchen floor?

I screamed. The mouse fell over a bit.

I screamed again. The mouse didn't move...

The saga continued.

ORGANIZATION IS NOT MY FORTE

Are you one of those organized people that I've heard about, the ones who always know where something is when they need it, even when they're in a rush? Are you able to find your car keys, your favorite beach bag, or the key to the fire-safe chest you store at the back of your bedroom closet?

If you can, you probably won't understand the painful process I'm going through trying to become even just a little bit like you.

I am not at all organized, but I want to change.

I don't like having plastic ware fall out of my cupboards every time I open them to search for a container and matching lid.

I get frustrated when I can't find the key to the garden shed or the battery charger for my cell phone, and I hate being late for an appointment because I can't locate the all-important document I need to take with me.

But being organized doesn't come naturally to me.

Apparently I'm a natural born pack-rat, as was my husband (although he was even **much** more so).

The consequence of having two pack-rats live together for almost 40 years was that we accumulated a LOT of stuff, and it's that stuff that's threatening to overtake my house now and send me running, screaming, to the nearest PRA (Pack-Ratter's Anonymous) meeting.

So I've considered my options and have decided that the only sane thing for me to do is to tackle my problem head-on. It's time for me to get organized.

But where do I start?

How do I decide what to keep, what to give away, what to toss?

The shows on TV make it look easy—choose a room, take everything out of the room, and put every single thing into one of three piles—keep, give away, throw.

Simple. Easy-peasy.

But that's my problem; to me it's not easy.

With which room should I begin—the one with the most stuff or the one with the least? And how exactly do I decide what to keep, what to give away or sell, and what to toss in the trash?

If I knew how to make these important decisions I probably wouldn't be in this mess in the first place!

And what do I do with the items I can't even identify—just because I don't know what something is or what it's for doesn't mean it isn't vital to the well-being of my home. Otherwise why would my husband have bought it and brought it home in the first place?

I have many unidentifiable items around my place, especially in the garage and shed and in my husband's workshop, and for now I've decided it's best to just leave those rooms alone.

There will be plenty of time to tackle them in the fall or next spring or in 2020.

For now I'm going to concentrate on organizing a room where I actually know what everything is for and if the things I find there really belong.

I'll begin with my kitchen.

***

Last week I bought a few items to help me organize my kitchen space: a divider that holds and separates baking sheets; a pull-out wire basket that hopefully will corral some of my plastic containers and lids; and a shelf that makes it possible to stack plates in two piles, one on top of the other, without having to lift up all the plates to reach the microwave safe ones I need for reheating last night's leftovers.

These small changes I'm making may seem like baby steps to a person who is naturally organized, but to me these changes are more like the "giant steps" in the game of "Simon Says" we played as children.

Who knew I would be able to grab a pizza pan from the cupboard under the wall oven without having all the other pans around it fall over?

This is the stuff of miracles; this is the stuff that makes day-to-day living easier and probably helps keep sane people sane.

Since I implemented these few changes in my kitchen I've discovered that I like being organized, and I want more of it.

I'm determined that a neat and tidy home will not just be a mirage in the distant horizon tantalizing me, but will instead be the serene oasis I long for at the end of an exhausting, thirsty day.

So my journey towards organization will continue.

But first, I think I'll bake something. Now that I've organized my baking cupboard I can actually retrieve the pans I need without any clattering and cursing, and I have easy access to the flour and sugar that most recipes call for. I wonder what I should bake....hmmm.

Would anyone care for a banana muffin? They're really delicious, and these ones were baked in actual muffin pans; they're much more appealing than the ones I spooned onto cookie sheets last week.

Ah, organization...how I do hope you stick with me forever.

OLD DOG, NEW TRICKS

Recently I decided that I want to learn to play a musical instrument, and after a lot of searching I finally found the perfect one for me.

Originally I had thought it would be fun to play a fiddle and be the popular person whenever family and friends gathered.

I would tune my fiddle and rosin up my bow and deliver foot-stomping, hand-clapping renditions of some well-known fiddle tunes while my family and friends oohed and aahed at my amazing ability to make my fiddle sing.

Then my sister-in-law decided to learn to play the fiddle, and I had the opportunity to watch her and listen to her practice, hour after hour, day after day.

It only took hearing her practice the fiddle once for me to realize that I would NEVER attempt such a feat as that; if I had to hear that screeching, howling, banshee-noise in my ears every day for an hour or more I knew that I would end up throwing the fiddle, the bow, the rosin, the sheet music and the fiddle case into the nearest trash bin and would likely light the trash bin on fire just to ensure that everything in it disappeared forever!

I simply do not have the patience or discipline required to learn such a temperamental musical instrument.

So, what then?

Well, maybe I could learn to play guitar. A lot of people I know play the guitar--how difficult could it be? Only six strings to master and surely I could manage a few chords on it.

But a guitar is big and the case to carry it around in is even bigger...did I want to lug that instrument from my house to my car to my cottage to my car to my house?

I don't think so.

Then my smarty-pants sister-in-law, Faye, suggested a ukulele.

Hmm, I liked that idea; a ukulele is small and only has four strings.

A ukulele it would be!

Faye had bought a tenor ukulele in the summer and plays it in a band in which she and my brother are members.

They call themselves the "Silver Birch Minstrels" and play every few weeks at a local senior's lodge in Alberta.

They have six band members (counting the older gentleman from the lodge, who plays the spoons), and between them they sing, play guitars, ukulele, banjo, drums, spoons, and bodhran (an Irish frame drum).

They play a variety of tunes from traditional to country to folksong to gospel, and Faye projects the song lyrics onto a screen so the residents can sing along with the band.

I think it's great that they're giving back to their community by spending time and energy entertaining seniors, but I don't expect that's something I'd ever be able to do.

I just want to play music for my own enjoyment.

So before I returned home from visiting my brother and sister-in-law, Faye and I shopped for the perfect instrument for me.

We did our online research first and found a music store that had a variety of ukuleles to try out—who knew there were so many options when it came to buying such a tiny instrument?

There are soprano ukes, concert ukes, tenor ukes and baritone ukes. There are ~~cheap~~ inexpensive ukuleles and ~~outrageously priced~~ quite expensive ones.

After some deep thought I decided to try a concert-sized ukulele, and Faye and I narrowed my choices down to two models.

The one I decided to buy was the more expensive of the two, but I love the sound it makes, it comes with its own case, it is thinner than the other one I tried and is very light-weight and easy to transport. Its top is solid spruce and its sides and back are mahogany veneer; it is indeed a handsome ukulele.

Now I just have to learn to play it.

***

I downloaded ukulele songs for my iPad2, and Faye gave me copies of songs she put together for The Silver Birch Minstrels. I also have a ukulele chord chart, and my son lent me one of his guitar tuners, so I have no excuse now not to learn to play at least a few chords.

I've been practicing every day since I came home from Alberta and I can now actually make a few recognizable sounds come out of this little beast, so that's a start, I guess.

The fingertips on my left hand are numb, as if they are filled with pins and needles, but I'm told this is a good thing–apparently it means I'm developing calluses on them and they eventually won't hurt as much when I press down on the frets. (I hope that happens soon because the strings now leave deep welts in my fingertips after just a few minutes of practice.)

I'm sure I will need a bit of luck along with my grit and determination to master a musical instrument at this stage in my not-so-young-anymore life, but I'm going to try my best to succeed.

I've heard that it's never too late to teach an old dog new tricks and I'm counting on that to be true as I tackle this instrument, but if this doesn't work out for me, if I find that after several weeks or months of practice people still can't recognize anything I'm playing on the ukulele, I will revert to my back-up plan...

When I was at the music store buying my ukulele, I noticed they also had 'wazoos' for sale, and I bought one for my son.

Until I saw one in the store I didn't even realize there was such a thing as a wazoo–I thought it was only a word made up to use in the expression, "Blow it out your big wazoo", but it is a real instrument–a kazoo with a little horn attached to it, so it actually ends up being a VERY LOUD kazoo!

I love it! And surely if I practice every day eventually I'll be able to hum into it and make some kind of sound come out.

Maybe I'll end up becoming multi-talented and will learn to play both the ukulele and the wazoo–just imagine how popular I'll be at family gatherings then!

I could even perform at weddings or anniversary parties or the Oscars.

Or maybe not.

But even if I eventually learn to play the ukulele or the kazoo just enough to amuse myself, this old dog will be a happy old dog.

And happy old dogs are surely the best!

I HAVE MET THE ENEMY, AND SHE IS MOSQUITO

I'm being brazen today, not only borrowing a well-known expression, but ~~corrupting~~ paraphrasing it as well.

My online research shows that the original sentence: "We have met the enemy and he is us," was first penned by Walt Kelly, author of a comic strip character named Pogo, for an **Earth Day poster in 1970.**

I checked with Wikipedia and it states that the comic strip, Pogo, often engaged in social and political satire, so I'm hoping that the late Walt would understand and would forgive me for using his phrase for my own twisted commentary on my sad little life.

I wouldn't do it if I wasn't desperate.

***

My house is under attack by mosquitoes.

And not just any mosquitoes, but the angry, female, 'have to have blood for my ovaries and eggs' kind of mosquitoes.

I have no idea where the male mosquitoes are or what they're up to while their female counterparts wage war against me, but I recently read that the males are, 'sensitive vegetarians', content to fly around and suck nectar and juices out of plants.

Way to go, wimpy male mosquitoes, way to go!

And I have to wonder why, after all these millions of years of development (I read that mosquitoes were around even during the dinosaur period), would the female mosquitoes not have figured out a way to lay their eggs WITHOUT needing to first feed on animals and people who never did anything to them! (*Unless you count the fact that we swat at them and spray their breeding sites in an attempt to annihilate their species.*)

And if the male mosquitoes are indeed 'sensitive vegetarians', why don't the female mosquitoes just suck some blood out of them?

They'd likely give it up willingly, just pausing for a few seconds on their way to the nearest flower garden or vegetable patch for a refill of nectar.

Why can't we all just get along?

Why do I have to make a run, keys in hand, for my front door, try to fling open the screen door, unlock the main door, open the main door, dash inside and desperately try to close the screen door before any mosquitoes join me inside (which is difficult to do because the door is on some kind of a hinge-thingy that won't allow it to close quickly)?

Why am I forced to be a prisoner in my own home, afraid to spend time in the yard or on my back deck where my arms and legs become mosquito buffet lines?

Why are mosquitoes so attracted to me?

Why won't they leave me alone?

Researchers have said that mosquitoes like certain blood types and that some people have more cholesterol and urea on their skin than do others, so maybe I'm one of those people…

I don't know. Apparently there are a lot of things I don't know about mosquitoes.

An article on DiscoverMagazine.com is titled "20 Things You Didn't Know About…Mosquitoes", and after reading the article I realized that of the 20 things it lists that I didn't know, there wasn't one thing that would help me in my struggle against this ravenous insect.

For example, while it is interesting to find out that **there are mosquitoes everywhere, from the Arctic tundra to the tropical rain forests**, I don't really care—I only care that there are mosquitoes in my yard, trying to get at my body and get into my home (and into my car). And there are mosquitoes in my cottage yard, trying to get at my body and get into my cottage (and into my car).

***

Yesterday I decided to do some planting in my front yard, and before I donned my garden gloves I made a trip to the laundry room, found a dryer sheet made for softening clothes, rubbed it over my arms and legs and neck, and then tucked it into a pocket of my shorts.

I had read somewhere that dryer sheets protect people against mosquito bites.

It didn't work for me at all, but I did smell pretty good, like fresh laundry on a warm summer day…fresh laundry covered with mosquitoes, sucking away on my arms and legs and neck.

Last weekend I visited a local nursery and bought four lemon geraniums (P. Citrosa) that are reputed to repel mosquitoes and black flies.

I planted all four new plants in handsome containers and placed the containers around the front door to my home.

It turns out that the mosquitoes love them, and just before I'm being bitten I've even heard them whispering about how great the entrance to my house looks and smells.

I'm hoping that as the plants grow and I continue to brush their leaves every time I dash in and out of my home they will begin to do what they're supposed to do and keep those pesky insects away from that particular spot.

In the meantime, though, I'm going to continue my search for other deterrents.

I've read that garlic may work, so I guess I could sprinkle garlic powder around my door and yard, but I'm afraid that my entire place would then just end up smelling like a lovely salad and would attract even more unwanted visitors.

When I was scouring the World Wide Web I also learned a few more facts about mosquitoes: did you know there are over 2700 species of mosquitoes worldwide? (So I doubt we really stand a chance against them in the long run, unless we wipe ourselves out in the fight, too).

And did you know that after a female mosquito mates, digests a blood meal and lays eggs, she again seeks a blood meal so that she can produce a second batch of eggs? Depending on her stamina and the weather, she may repeat this process many times without mating again.

Finally, I should tell you about my late husband, Gary, who was ever-diligent in his fight to eliminate the flying hordes.

He used to come home with every imaginable type of mosquito repellent known to man (and woman), including machines run by electricity and ones run by propane, and he set them up around the yard and tended to them faithfully.

But one of the favorite stories my children and I tell of him is the day he came home with a new prized possession--the "Exterminator"--an electronic bug zapper that resembled a red badminton racquet.

Gary was like a little boy who had just been given a new toy; he was so happy to be able to strike out at the insects that attacked him and his family, and he wasted no time trying out this new weapon.

The first afternoon he had the Exterminator he took a leisurely walk around our yard.

I could hear his progress from inside the house, just by listening to the "zip, zip, zip" sounds coming from outside.

I'm sure Gary walked around every inch of our property, swinging the racquet and electrifying mosquitoes left and right and center, returning to the house a very happy man.

He bragged that buying the Exterminator was the best $30 he ever spent in his life (except, I'm sure, for my engagement ring...but I digress).

And even though I really miss the sound of Gary zapping away at mosquitoes, the memory of him doing so still brings a smile to my face.

There you have it--my sorry tale of trying to outwit creatures that have been around much longer than my species. That fact alone should be enough to tell me that I'll never win this war.

I should likely admit defeat now, sign up for an online movie source and barricade myself into my home until October.

Now That I'm Mature

Because once the frost hits, the mosquitoes leave; mind you, once the frost hits, the snow arrives...

I can't seem to win.

OH WHERE, OH WHERE, DID MY LITTLE PENDANT GO?

Once again you'll have to forgive me for changing yet another famous line to suit my own pathetic purposes.

This time I've chosen the beginning of a well-known nursery rhyme/song "Oh Where, Oh Where, Has My Little Dog Gone" in order to share with you my sad tale of losing something that means a great deal to me.

This week I lost a diamond pendant.

I tried to make myself feel better by saying that I didn't really **lose** it; I simply misplaced it.

Then I realized I misplaced it so well that I couldn't find it anywhere, so for all intents and purposes my diamond necklace was indeed lost.

Now, I'm not accustomed to draping myself in diamonds, but I do cherish the ones I have because they were gifts from my late husband, Gary, and that really makes them special to me.

For example, this pendant was originally a ring that Gary won at a charity fund-raiser his local Rotary club held one year.

I was totally surprised when he arrived home with it the night of the event, and I was even more surprised when I slipped it on my right ring finger and it fit perfectly.

And there it stayed for several years.

Then in 2009 Gary and I were browsing in a jewelry store when he spied a gorgeous one carat white-gold diamond ring and called me over to have a look. (He told me later that as soon as he saw that particular ring he knew we weren't going to leave the store without it.)

"It looked like you," he said, and he wanted me to have it.

How could I possibly argue with logic like that?

While we were negotiating price the store owner noticed the yellow-gold ring on my right hand, and to seal our deal, he offered to reset it in a white-gold pendant for me at no extra cost.

So my yellow-gold diamond ring became my white gold diamond pendant, and the white gold diamond ring from the jewelry store display case became mine.

Both pieces of jewelry hold great sentimental value to me; when I wear them I am reminded of my husband and of the wonderful love and life we shared for over thirty-seven years.

My diamond ring comes off only to be cleaned, and I wear the pendant most of the time too, so it was a mystery to me when I discovered it wasn't around my neck where it usually hung.

It was a Tuesday afternoon and I was already running late; I should have left home by one fifteen in order to meet friends in Amherst (a nearby town), by one thirty, but it was already one fifteen when I went into my bedroom to change my clothes.

I had just donned a pair of turquoise capris from my closet and pulled on a white short-sleeved cotton sweater to go with it when I noticed that I was no longer wearing my diamond pendant.

I mentally retraced my steps...

I had arrived home from my cottage on Monday morning to visit with a friend and her grand-baby who dropped in for a visit.

I had held the sweet little six-month-old while she grabbed at my glasses and my nose and my tank top with her chubby little baby-hands—did she grab at my necklace too, and perhaps eat it without either her grandma or me noticing?

I didn't think that was possible, but babies can be wily so I didn't rule it out one hundred percent.

I also remembered that after my friend and her granddaughter left I washed my hair in the bathroom sink because another friend was dropping in for a visit and I didn't think I'd have time to shower.

Did the pendant chain break when I had my head stuck in the sink—did I wash it down the drain along with the shampoo and rinse water?

I checked the sink, checked the bathroom cabinet and floor, checked the tub (I hadn't even been in the tub so I have no idea why I looked there, but I did).

No pendant.

Perhaps the chain did break.

Recently I had replaced the pendant's sturdy sterling silver chain with a delicate white-gold one because the silver chain reacted with my skin and cleaning the tarnish off it (the chain, not my skin), had become impossible to do.

Maybe the new chain I bought was too flimsy to hold such a precious stone—why hadn't I spent the extra money on a much stronger chain—like the ones I sometimes see wrapped around truck tires in the winter?

***

Although it meant that I would be very late meeting my friends in Amherst I decided that I had to take the time to look for my pendant.

I looked in my house, I looked in my car, and I looked in the yard around my house and my car.

No pendant.

I found lots of dust-bunnies in my house, I found leaves and twigs and rocks in my car, and I found mosquitoes and more mosquitoes in my yard, but I didn't find my pendant.

I finally gave up my search and headed to Amherst, pendant-less and very upset.

It was late afternoon when I arrived back home.

I came into the house, preparing to do my "CSI" routine, the one where investigators use flashlights to search for clues.

I opened the cupboard to retrieve my favorite flashlight—a big shiny black one that could pinpoint a hummingbird on a neighbor's feeder 200 yards away—when my son came home from work and offered to help me search.

We decided to start in my bedroom again.

I pulled back the quilt and the bed sheets and looked under the pillows; my son searched the floor by the bed.

Then I glanced at my dresser and spied the case that the new chain had come in and where I usually stored my pendant whenever I did take it off.

Wouldn't that be weird, I thought, *if all this time the pendant had been tucked away in its case.* And although I knew it wouldn't be there, I decided I'd better check it out anyway.

Imagine my immense surprise and my even more immense feelings of stupidity when I snapped open the case and revealed my necklace, nestled safe and sound in the velvet-lined box.

I felt particularly foolish that I had searched high and low for my necklace before checking the case on my dresser, and I still don't remember placing the pendant inside that case, but I am very relieved that I found it.

Can I still say it was lost if the entire time it was actually where it was supposed to be?

But it did feel lost to me, so I suppose that is what counts here, not the semantics of when is something lost or when is something not lost. My pendant was lost to me and then it was found.

Good news.

And I am somewhat consoled by knowing that I am not the only middle-aged person who loses things lately.

My brother, Les, visited recently from Alberta, and when he headed to the airport for his return flight home he was forced to leave without a pair of his glasses. He had misplaced them **somewhere** in my house, and even though we searched for an hour or more the morning he left, we couldn't find them.

I still haven't found them.

But Les did tell me that when I do find then, I'll probably find his pen-knife too, as it is also missing.

Another friend of mine can't find the keys to her fire-safe chest—she and her husband have searched for them for months now and are just about ready to give up and call a locksmith.

And one day recently another friend couldn't find her purse when she arrived at the grocery store checkout; she retraced her steps from the checkout, up and down the store aisles and finally back to her car. There was her purse, on the front seat, grinning, I think.

Another time this same friend tried to return bed pillows to a department store and became very upset with the clerk when she told her that she couldn't accept the return.

My friend demanded to know why the pillows couldn't be returned--they were still in their plastic covers and she had a receipt, she said.

The clerk bent close to her, doing her best to avoid an embarrassing scene, and whispered, "Our company doesn't sell that particular brand of pillow, and the receipt in your hand is actually from a competitor's place."

My good friend smiled meekly and thanked the nice clerk then beat a hasty retreat to the nearest exit.

So yes, it's nice to know that I'm not alone in my sometimes-fog; it's nice to know that other people over the age of fifty are also forgetful.

It's nice to know that I'm not the only one who wonders why I walked into a room and then to retrace my steps to figure it out, or why I buy a magazine and discover, once I begin to read the $8.95 (plus tax), treasure at home, that the articles seem vaguely familiar, only to find the exact same magazine, that I bought a week or two earlier, tucked into my bedside table drawer.

So the next time I'm home from the cottage I'm going to search again for my brother's glasses; I'll use my trusty

"CSI" flashlight to peer into room corners and underneath sofas, and I won't give up until I'm successful.

I think I'll start by looking in the guest bedroom, on the dresser, where my brother usually placed his spectacles at night before falling asleep.

Who knows—I may just be surprised again.

UP, UP AND AWAY

Last week, while I was visiting family members in Alberta, I had the opportunity to take a hot-air balloon ride (and before any of you wise-crackers out there--and you know who you are--suggest that I could have powered that balloon with just MY hot-air, let me assure you there were several propane gas cylinders involved in this particular hot-air balloon excursion, and I was only a passenger)!

The morning that we were supposed to soar through the air dawned clear and cool. We left the house just after 5:30 AM to head to the pick-up site because we were supposed to be there, bright-eyed and bushy-tailed, by 6:45 AM and it was quite a long drive into that part of the city.

We arrived in plenty of time and anxiously awaited the flight crew's arrival (doesn't that sound as if we were preparing to head to the moon in a space shuttle?).

The crew arrived in a van, hauling the balloon's basket behind it in a trailer.

We gathered around the pilot like fans seeking an autograph from a famous rock star, but alas, he had bad news for us.

"I'm sorry to have to tell you this, folks," he said, "but there doesn't seem to be enough wind to fly this morning."

Our group of would-be-balloonists was surprised.

I had worried about all sorts of problems with the flight—thunder and lightning, a heavy rainstorm, too much wind....but had never considered the possibility that there might not be enough wind.

I learned something new that day--hot-air balloons can't take off if there isn't enough wind current to move them along at a certain speed. But that knowledge wasn't a whole lot of solace for my brother, sister-in-law and me as we drove back home that morning.

Fortunately, my sister-in-law Faye was able to re-book our flight for the following Tuesday and we were optimistic that we would really soar like the birds before I had to head back to New Brunswick later that week.

The next Tuesday we were up again before the sun and drove back to the pick-up site near one of the city's zoos.

The weather looked promising; the morning was sunny and there was a light breeze. Fingers crossed.

When we arrived at the site and saw three balloons already in the air we knew the odds of actually getting off the ground were stacking up in our favor.

Two crews arrived in vans, each one hauling a trailer holding a large wicker basket, although one basket was much larger than the other. We learned that the small basket only held two passengers and the pilot, and a young-and-in-love couple had reserved that particular basket for themselves.

Rumor had it that the young man had originally planned to propose to his girlfriend high above the earth, but their first few attempts at ballooning were canceled and he finally decided to propose on land and go up in the balloon whenever air currents and fate allowed.

It's too bad it didn't work out the way the young man had planned, but I'm sure the engagement ring he placed on his fiancée's finger a week or so before their flight really sparkled in the early morning sunlight.

***

There were eight of us going up in our balloon, but first we piled into the van and drove to an open field where the crew laid the balloon (attached to the basket by ropes), out on the ground to be inflated.

Once the balloon was ready the crew tipped the basket upright again—it had been lying on its side while the balloon was being inflated--and then the pilot told each of us where we should stand when we climbed into the basket.

There were six compartments in all—the pilot and the balloon's equipment took up the middle two compartments and there were two more compartments on each end of the basket.

My sister-in-law and I were paired together, and my brother and another man shared the compartment right beside ours, so all was good.

But getting into the basket was a challenge for me.

There were two foot-holds for feet; a person was supposed to step up into the left one then swing his or her right leg and foot up to the higher one and then somehow gracefully swing the left leg and then the right over the top of the basket and descend like a feather into the tiny compartment below.

I am not graceful, I am not a feather, and I am not good at climbing anything! I have 'bad' knees that tend to buckle on me when they are bent and trying to support my ~~considerable~~ bird-like weight, so getting my body into the basket was similar to trying to ease a fully-awake cat into a tub full of water.

No cooperation, no matter how many times it's tried.

Finally, my brother and a member of the crew hoisted me up like a very big bag of potatoes and kind of heaved me over the side of the basket, where I landed like a…well, like a very big bag of potatoes. But at least I was in the basket and ready to go. The other passengers gracefully descended into the basket and we all turned expectantly to the pilot.

Thumbs up, everyone!

Our balloon then took flight--first just a few tentative feet above the ground, then higher and higher over the tree tops.

Cameras clicked and we passengers smiled, happy to be away from the mosquitoes that had pestered us in the field.

We flew over parks, a golf course, residential streets and the city center airport.

This experience was very different than flying in a plane; even when I saw the world through the windows of a small single-engine plane my brother used to fly, it was not comparable to floating over the city in a hot-air balloon.

I turned my face to the sun and felt a gentle breeze in my hair, but there was very little noise.

Other than the occasional sound from the propane cylinder that kept the balloon inflated, the ride was quiet. In fact, it was almost eerily quiet.

I could hear dogs barking below us and car horns honking at each other in the distance, but that was all.

If I had to describe the balloon ride in just one word, I would say it was 'peaceful'. Not exhilarating, not exciting even, or scary…just peaceful.

I can imagine, though, before air-travel became commonplace, the thrill that passengers in the hot-air balloons experienced when they lifted off from the earth and viewed the world from hundreds of feet above the ground for the first time.

***

After fifty minutes or so of drifting in the wind, our pilot began to search for a safe place to land. He decided on a field far off in the distance, and we headed that way.

A few minutes later it was time to prepare ourselves for landing. The pilot instructed us to face forward, slightly bend our knees, grip the padded railing and hold on.

The field came towards us quickly, and we actually brushed against a treetop as we neared the chosen location.

The field itself was empty, except for soccer goalposts and one lone bench.

The pilot spoke. "Are you all familiar with Murphy's Law," he asked, "where anything that can go wrong will go wrong?"

Eight heads bobbed up and down.

"Well, I think we're going to hit that bench down there," he said.

And we did.

Our basket grazed the bench and bounced off it to the ground, sliding several meters before finally coming to a full stop in the field.

When our basket slid over the grass, which was still wet with early-morning dew, it disturbed thousands of mosquitoes that were hiding or sleeping or mating there. (Who actually knows what mosquitoes do in the early morning hours?)

Whatever the mosquitoes were doing, they were not happy being disturbed, and they immediately swarmed us.

Sixteen arms and hands swatted at them while we took turns climbing out of the basket.

I'll spare you the details of my exit from the basket to the ground; just trust me when I say that it wasn't graceful or pretty and it required the help of a crew member.

But finally I managed to extricate myself from the basket and stand upright in the field, swatting at mosquitoes while doing my best to hold onto the basket to help keep it from becoming airborne again as the other passengers descended from it.

Once the crew deflated the balloon and loaded the equipment back onto the trailer we piled into the van and drove to a more-or-less mosquito-free area where we then stopped to enjoy a glass of champagne--an honored tradition in the hot air balloon world to celebrate a successful flight.

The pilot handed out lapel pins and flight certificates, and then drove us back to where our excursion began, near the zoo.

We shook hands with fellow passengers, said our good-byes to the crew and headed to the car.

Our hot-air balloon adventure was officially over.

We were fortunate that the weather cooperated with us that morning, and we were able to go up in the balloon on only our second attempt.

One fellow passenger told us that he had tried nine previous times without success and was about ready to give up, so I'm glad that the number ten turned out to be his lucky number.

As difficult as it was to give up my cozy bed at five in the morning, it was worth it to be able to say that I've done something new, something that I've never done before and likely will never do again, and to report that I survived to talk about it.

Next on my list of things to do is to take a helicopter ride over an active volcano in Hawaii this November.

I really hope that a helicopter is easy to climb into and that there are no mosquitoes around when we land.

I'll let you know if my luck holds.

WHAT I HAD NOT PLANNED TO DO ON MY VACATION

Last week I took a mini-vacation, hoping to enjoy September's warm days and cool nights that are so prevalent in my little corner of the world.

I had plans to write, to houseclean, to hang a few pictures in my living room and to relax on the swing in my gazebo with a good book and a glass of wine.

I didn't have plans to go to my local hospital's emergency department in severe pain halfway through my vacation week; I didn't plan to be poked and prodded and x-rayed and spend the night in the hospital on pain killers, but that's what happened.

I didn't plan to go by ambulance to a larger hospital in a nearby city the next morning and to once again be poked and prodded and injected for a CT (computed tomography) abdominal scan before having an emergency appendectomy Thursday evening, but that's what happened.

I didn't plan to have difficulty breathing in-and-out in the recovery room, to subsequently be injected with a drug that reversed all the effects of the pain-killing drugs I'd been given previously, and to have all pain-killing drugs withheld from me for several more hours until my breathing stabilized.

But that's exactly what happened.

***

I was not a surgery-virgin; I'd seen my share of operating rooms, and I truly thought I was intimate with pain, but I had never experienced pain to the degree that I did that Thursday night.

This was strong, expert pain from the seven-inch horizontal incision that the surgeon sliced into my abdominal tissue and muscle in his hunt for my elusive inflamed appendix, and I couldn't be given any drugs, not even ibuprofen or acetaminophen to help me cope.

When I was taken from recovery and wheeled back to my hospital room, the nurses helping me back onto my bed apologized to my husband and son, saying they knew it looked and sounded as if they were torturing me, but that they had no choice.

They said they couldn't risk depressing my breathing again.

So I suffered through several painfully-long, agonizing hours.

It's probably a good thing nobody asked for my opinion at that time--I would have said that I'd gladly take my chances with the drugs...

After four or five hours I finally received an injection—not a full dose, not even half a dose, but a quarter dose, enough to slightly take the edge off my pain and allow me to think that I might actually survive the night, allow me to think that I might actually **want** to survive the night.

***

Around three in the morning my husband and son went home for some rest, and I spent the remainder of my night counting the hours, minutes and seconds between my last pain injection and my next one.

During that time I also practiced my breathing; I figured if I forgot how to do it once I might forget again so I wanted to keep up-to-date with the technique.

To complicate things further, by five o'clock Friday morning the intravenous liquids and antibiotics that were pumping through my veins had filled my bladder to capacity and I simply had to relieve the intense pressure that was building up in my abdomen.

My nurse said I had two choices: use a bedpan or attempt a trip to the bathroom that was several meters away from my bed.

Neither option appealed to me, but I hadn't travelled in a while, so decided a trip to the bathroom was in order.

I gripped the bed's side rail and rolled partway onto my left side, then with the nurse's help I hoisted myself semi-upright and slid my legs over the side of the bed.

Perspiration ran down my body, my abdomen burned like fire from hell, and I still wasn't anywhere near the bathroom.

After a minute or two of deep breathing (fortunately I had practiced this in the night), I struggled to my feet, and the nurse, my IV pole and I wobbled to the washroom.

It was five-fifteen when I fell back into my bed, exhausted and drenched with perspiration.

By the time breakfast arrived at eight o'clock I had been without food or drink, other than a few sips of tepid water in the night, for thirty-six hours.

The nurse told me that I was on a "Clear Liquid" diet, so I knew not to expect anything good on my meal trays that first post-surgery day.

And I was correct. Breakfast consisted of black coffee, apple juice and lemon gelatin. Lunch was black tea, clear chicken broth, orange sherbet and lemon gelatin. Supper was a clone of lunch, except the orange sherbet was replaced with lime sherbet.

Variety is, after all, the spice of life.

I hesitate to give gelatin any more time in the spotlight than necessary so will quickly explain reasons one to one hundred why it should never, ever be served to a post-surgery patient, and why it should especially never, ever be served to **this** post-surgery patient.

Reason 1—Gelatin is a vile, despicable substance derived from collagen (think protein) found inside animal bone, cartilage, tendon and other connective tissue. A bit of fruit flavor is added to this semi-solid mass before it appears on meal trays, but trust me, a touch a fruit does not an edible dessert make.

Reason 2-100—See **Reason 1** above.

Fortunately for me, I didn't have any appetite on Friday, but even if I'd been famished, the lone remnant of untouched food on my tray would have been, will always be... any and every flavor of gelatin known to mankind.

Nothing more really needs to be said.

***

The surgeon dropped in around nine o'clock that morning and had a quick peek at my incision—he said it looked good. He also said he felt bad for me because he had to cut through so much muscle during the operation that I would be sore for a long time.

He said I should be able to go home in two or three days and he wanted to see me in his office in six weeks.

For the next few days, though, my home-away-from-home was this semi private room, near the nurse's station and the patient lounge.

I occupied Bed B, next to the window. The view wasn't great—another brick-walled wing of the hospital, but at least I could see the sun and didn't feel claustrophobic the way I might if I had occupied Bed A, closer to the door and the bathroom.

Bed A was currently empty and I looked forward to a peaceful, quiet day in which to rest and begin my recovery.

By ten AM my visions of peace and quiet lay shattered, like an heirloom china teacup dropped onto a ceramic tile floor.

Loud voices outside my room, annoying music from a television game show in the patient lounge, banging and clanging of linen carts and medicine carts being pushed up and down the hall, whirring noises from a ride-on floor polisher doing its best to get on my one last nerve…this was not what the doctor ordered!

How could anyone rest and recover amid this cacophony of sounds?

My pain medication had been increased to half a regular dose every four hours, enough to manage the pain for about two hours out of the four, leaving me in full-blown misery for the remaining two hours between doses.

I became a watcher of clocks, carefully planning what I had to do within that small window of time when my pain was under control—that's when I would wobble along on my mandatory walk, make a trip to the bathroom, brush my hair or teeth, and sit in a chair.

I quickly established a routine—receive the needle, lie quietly until the narcotic released its magical powers, do whatever it was I had to do and be back in bed, attempting to sleep or at the very least to lie completely still for the last one hundred and twenty minutes until the cycle could begin again.

Friday afternoon my husband and son arrived for a visit and shortly afterwards, so did my daughter and her boyfriend. I was happy to see them and to have them spend time with me, but I certainly wasn't a good hostess.

I was so tired that I had to close my eyes every few minutes and just lie there, mutely listening to the conversation around me.

***

By late afternoon a woman named Patty, also fresh from abdominal surgery, moved into the room to occupy Bed A.

Patty had her own pain and recovery to deal with, and I could certainly appreciate that.

We introduced ourselves but kept the curtain between us fully drawn that evening, respecting each other's need for privacy.

That night, though, as I rattled back and forth to the washroom for my hourly trips, wheeling my I.V. buddy with me like a tall, skinny giraffe on a leash, I realized how much noise I was making, and I apologized to Patty for disturbing her.

She told me that I hardly disturbed her at all because she wore ear-plugs at night to cut out external sounds—for the next few nights that would be the hospital noises that never go away, and for all other nights of her life it was her husband's snoring.

That night I was finally allowed have a full dose of pain medication, and oh, what a world of difference it made to me, to my body's ability to cope with the trauma it had been through.

At last I was able to stay fairly comfortable between my four-hour injections.

***

Saturday morning…breakfast arrived while I was in the washroom, but through the closed door I heard the unmistakable sound of trays being delivered to our room.

What culinary delights await me? I wondered, as I washed my hands.

My stomach growled in anticipation of an actual meal—eggs perhaps, a rasher of bacon, hot buttered toast with strawberry jam, coffee with cream…

"What do you have for breakfast?" I asked Patty as I came out of the bathroom. "Is it real food?"

Patty lifted the plastic cover off her plate and revealed a boiled egg and toast. She also had oatmeal, orange juice, and coffee. It all looked delicious.

I hobbled past Patty's bed to mine.

There on my bed table sat my meal tray--sad, lonely, almost empty…no boiled egg or toast with strawberry jam to be seen. Only black coffee, apple juice, and red gelatin!

Why is the world such a cruel, cruel place, I wondered. *What did I do to deserve this punishment?*

Fortunately for me, a Florence Nightingale-nurse appeared on the scene, took one look at the lack of food on my tray and said, "We can't have that; I'm sure the doctor meant for you to have solid foods today. I'll go make you a slice of toast. Would that be good?"

I began to drool, exactly like one of Pavlov's dogs.

"That would be wonderful," I panted.

Within a couple of minutes Florence returned with not one, but two slices of toast, a pat of butter, and two small containers of jam. What she didn't return with, however, was a knife, as she foolishly thought there would already be one on my tray, waiting to spread butter and jam and love on the lightly toasted bread.

So Ms Nightingale disappeared again and came back a moment later with a small white plastic knife.

I declared her to be a saint and began buttering, jamming (is that a word), and eating my two slices of toast, washing the delicious bites down with lukewarm black coffee.

I draped my napkin over the red gelatin, like a flag over a coffin, and vowed that if anyone ever served me gelatin again I would smear the goo all over the tray, the walls, my bed and myself, and would refuse to wash it off until I was given something edible in its place!

Thankfully I didn't have to implement that plan as my trays at lunch, supper and breakfast the next morning arrived *sans* gelatin.

In fact, Sunday morning I was treated to a boiled egg, toast with butter and jam, and coffee with cream. The food gods had heard my pleas and had listened.

Good for you, food gods!

Sunday morning was also a good morning for another reason.

The doctor on weekend duty came to my room and said that I could go home to recover as long as I followed the list of rules I would be given and looked after myself.

I promised I would, nodding my head at him like a bobble-dog in the back window of a car.

I still had to have two more doses of I.V. antibiotics before I could be discharged, but I figured I could handle that standing on my head if I had to.

I packed my meager belongings in a little bag, talked with Patty and her husband while I waited for the I.V. to finish dripping its healing liquids into my veins, and then changed from my hospital gown to a pair of lounge pants and a short sleeved t-shirt.

By this time I was exhausted, but I knew that once I arrived home I could sleep in my own cozy bed, in my own cozy nightgown, and I would wake up just in time to share a lovely supper with my family--supper that would not, by the way, include any sign of gelatin!

Nothing more really needs to be said.

RANDOM FRIDAY THOUGHTS

It's a rainy, windy day today and I find that my thoughts are jumbled too, as if they are also being buffeted about by an unseen gale.

So I've decided that today I'd capture some of the random thoughts and questions that circle around my brain, bouncing against the inside of my skull like pin-balls in an arcade machine.

***

I hope that people don't judge me when they find out about one of the guilty pleasures I've enjoyed since I retired: no matter what time of the morning I wake up *(it varies because I no longer use an alarm clock)*, I prop myself up on a couple of pillows then check my email and play a few games on my iPad2.

I wiggle my toes and enjoy the touch of the soft sheets against my skin, and sometimes I stay like this for an hour or more before I rise for the day.

***

When I'm in a rush to get somewhere in my town, why is it that all the snail-drivers in my town also decide it's time to be on the road?

Why can't they start their trips early in the morning if it's going to take them half an hour to drive a couple of kilometers through our not-so-busy town streets?

Why do they insist on being in the car just in front of my car, and why do they stop for every crack in the pavement and every caterpillar on the side of the road that they think might want to cross to the other side?

What makes them think that their snail-vehicles will only go twenty kilometers an hour? Why don't they walk if they have all this time to waste? Ahhh! Makes me crazy!

***

Every once in a while I pull up a YouTube video of Susan Boyle singing "*I Dreamed a Dream*", from her audition on Britain's Got Talent, and I play the video over and over again, singing my heart out along with her.

I love that video, and if I ever find out that it was staged in any way, I will be one very disappointed little woman.

Speaking of music videos that I love to watch and watch and watch, two of my favorites of all time are Leonard Cohen's *Live in London* and Eric Clapton's *Unplugged*. If you have never watched these fantastic performances you have missed out on audio and visual treats and you should correct that as soon as possible.

Other favorites of mine include The Band's *The Last Waltz*, and Ray Charles' *An Evening with Ray Charles*.

Come visit me sometime and we can watch these videos together; I'll even supply the wine.

***

Why do I have such vivid, weird dreams when I finally fall asleep at night? All I want is a few much-needed hours of restful sleep, but instead I dream...a lot.

Last night I dreamt of earth-invaders that came in human form *even though we knew they were alien*, and they took over our homes and our families.

In my dream one earth-invader *who bore a striking resemblance to Pierce Brosnan* set up house with a woman *who may or may not have been me*, and her children and a couple of dogs *although I think there were also beavers and muskrats involved somehow*.

The dream went on and on with some killing and zapping, and then the woman, *who may or may not have been me*, was finally stuck in the neck with a killing-needle *by the Pierce Brosnan look-alike*, before the telephone rang and woke me up.

Other nights I dream of ships, *involving a lot of line-ups and luggage mix-ups and being on the wrong plane or the wrong ship but trying to find my way to the right ship*, and I dream of hospitals, *where I am apparently working, although I never know what I'm supposed to be doing*.

I often dream of Gary, my deceased husband, and sometimes in my dreams he's alive and is with me, and sometimes he is with me and talks with me *even though I know, during the entire dream, that he isn't really alive*. All dreams of Gary leave me waking up sad, lonely and fervently wishing for him to be beside me again, even just for a little while.

***

I wonder about other things too.

Why do some people turn up their noses at wine that comes in boxes even though it's exactly the same wine that comes in bottles only you get more wine for your dollar and there is probably less packaging involved overall?

How come I can hear a song that I've never heard before and still guess, *usually quite accurately,* at the rhyming words there will be at the end of any given line? And if that is a special talent I have, why don't I write songs?

How far could my car actually travel without running out of gas once the 'gas light' comes on? One day I think I'll check this out—I'll put a full gas can in my trunk, and then I'll drive and drive until the car coasts to a stop, completely empty.

I'll track the kilometers/miles I'm able to drive and will let you know the results.

I'm sure this knowledge could come in handy one day when my car's gas light comes on but it's pouring rain and I don't want to stop, or it's snowing and I don't want to stop, or I just want to get home and I don't want to stop.

I'm sure it will prove to be a handy point of reference at some time in my future.

You may want to try this with your vehicle too, *unless you drive a snail-car, because if you do drive a snail-car you likely would never let the gas in your vehicle get low enough for the light to ever come on and you also probably never drive outside the town limits!*

***

Well, I see that the rain has stopped and the wind has died down and it's time to think about what I should do with my day.

Never mind that it's almost five PM—there are still plenty of hours left to practice my ukulele, watch a favorite DVD and maybe even toss a load of laundry into the washing machine.

This was fun, and cathartic somehow. I may have to do this again.

CRUISING TO HAWAII

Today my sister-in-law and I are boarding a cruise ship for a fourteen-day round trip voyage between Los Angeles and Hawaii.

Our plan is to relax our minds and bodies, recharge our emotional batteries and relish the feeling of not having a care in the world.

For two full weeks we won't have to worry about what to cook, where to go, or what to wear.

The hardest decision we'll have to make is which, if any, excursions we'll take on the four Hawaiian Islands we'll visit during our trip.

We discussed our options before we left our homes and we tentatively booked three excursions.

Our number one choice is a helicopter tour over a volcano—I've never been in a helicopter before but my sis-in-law, Faye, says that it's lots of fun and told me that I will really enjoy the experience.

We booked the tour for early in the morning on day five of our trip.

Our second choice is a submarine ride where we will experience an 'up-close-and-personal' look at the gorgeous corals and sea life that inhabit Hawaii's coastline and reefs.

I've never been in a submarine before but my sis-in-law says that it's lots of fun and that I will love it…so that excursion is also booked.

And last but not least we chose a snorkeling tour.

Now, I'm not a strong swimmer nor have I ever snorkeled before, but my sis-in-law says that it's lots of fun and that I will…wait a minute–I'm beginning to notice a trend here…

I may yet cancel that last adventure if I start to feel that tempting fate three times in a row is just downright foolish!

Faye and I also decided that we'd explore some of the local interests on our own, and the rest of the time we'd enjoy the ship's amenities, soak up the rejuvenating rays of the sun (covered in our 30 SPF sunblock, of course), and dip our pasty white bodies into refreshing pools.

And we'll snap pictures of our adventures.

I deleted most of the images from my camera's memory card in order to be able to click, click, click, and my sis-in-law bought a new camera that also can take pictures under water, so there's no reason we can't digitally capture all the highlights of our trip.

Then we'll be able to bore our friends and family for hours at a time when we return home.

Yay!

Okay…I must go for now…It's almost time for the shuttle to arrive at our hotel to transport us to the pier, and I want to make sure I have my suitcase ready. Please think of me on day five, in a helicopter, hovering over an active volcano…and keep your fingers and toes crossed.

HI HO, HAWAII

My Hawaiian cruise has been wonderful so far—even though Faye and I shared a cabin we have really gotten along and not once did she ~~try to smother me in my sleep~~ complain about my gentle snoring.

I did notice that she always wore earphones plugged into her iPod when she snuggled into her twin bed to settle for the night, but I'm sure that had nothing to do with me...

Back to the cruise: Our ship left Los Angeles, California on a Wednesday afternoon, and four-and-a-half-days later we arrived at Hilo, on the big island of Hawaii.

We had originally booked a helicopter tour for that island, but our cruise line cancelled all helicopter tours until an investigation could be completed into the latest crash where four tourists and the pilot were killed when their helicopter crashed into an Hawaiian mountainside.

I was sick to my stomach when I heard the news about the crash and felt terribly bad for all the people involved, but I had no desire to test the helicopter gods myself, so I was relieved that our cruise line took the decision away from me and cancelled the sponsored tours.

Instead, Faye and I booked a bus excursion to the Volcanoes National Park on the island of Hawaii.

After we lined up at the ship's terminal and boarded our bus, Leroy J, our ~~extremely talkative~~ informative driver, introduced himself and didn't stop narrating or commenting on the local sights and on Hawaiian facts for the next four hours.

Leroy J was from Wisconsin, *the cheese-state*, he said, but had come to Hawaii twenty-odd years ago and never looked back. *Wouldn't live anywhere else*, he said.

Leroy knew a lot about the island and about the weather—on one side of the island it's wet—rain-forest wet, while on the other side of the island it's dry—desert dry.

He knew all about Pele (not Pele the soccer player but Pele the goddess of Volcanoes), and he said that if Pele decided it was time for a volcano to erupt then there was nothing Leroy or anyone else could do about it except run out-of-the-way of the lava and fire.

He said his home, and most of the island homes, are built on stilts, so that if Pele becomes angry the homes can be cut away from the stilts with chainsaws, loaded onto flat-bed trucks and moved to a safe point on the island.

He said that if we ever see him, Leroy J, running down the road behind a flat-bed truck, that we'd better haul our butts into gear and start running, too!

I think that Leroy J can be ~~most politely~~ best described as being a *'character'*...

Once we entered the National Park we drove to the lookout point on Crater Rim Drive, where we could see volcanic gases rise from the Halema'uma'u Crater.

I snapped pictures of the crater, all the while thinking that the scene could have come straight out of the set of a science fiction movie or television series. Picture Star Trek 1960s television episodes...

Then we visited the Jaggar_Museum where we saw a variety of lava samples–from huge rocks to thin hair-like strands that are aptly called "Pele's Hair", and we visited the museum's gift shop, where I bought a beautiful 2012 calendar and a jigsaw_puzzle of a volcano that I hope to work on this winter.

Our tour of the park also included a stop at the Thurston Lava Tube, a cave-like structure left behind after lava from a volcano cooled and formed floors, walls, and a ceiling.

We walked along a rain-forest trail and down ~~thousands~~ many steps to descend into the tube where we followed other tourists through the near-darkness until we reached the tube's end.

Then it was up more steps and back along the trail to where our air-conditioned bus waited for us.

Oh joy, oh relief to feel a cool breeze on my face after the heat of the rain forest.

We left the park suitably impressed with the volcanic craters and the lava tube and highly recommend a visit to this little jut of rock in the Pacific Ocean.

Our bus tour with Leroy J was ~~long~~ great, but by the time we returned to the ship I was more than ready to get back to my routine. It had been ~~days~~ four hours since I'd eaten breakfast, and I was starved.

Leroy deposited us at the pier and we waved good-bye to the tour guide from *the Cheese State*, then snaked our way through the long security line and finally made it back onto our ship.

I was really anxious to change into my bathing suit and cool off with a relaxing dip in the pool, but first things first.

I swear I could actually hear the buffet calling my name.

LOSING MY SNORKELING
VIRGINITY

Our third stop during our recent Hawaiian cruise was on the island of Kauai, which is geologically the oldest of the main Hawaiian Islands.

This island is also aptly referred to as "The Garden Isle" because it is so lush and beautiful, and it was on this island that I lost my snorkeling virginity...

Soon after our ship docked at the port of Nawiliwili, Faye and I disembarked and found our tour group that would be going on the snorkeling adventure with us.

The port itself wasn't anything to write home about—from our balcony vantage point we mainly saw warehouses and gigantic transport trucks, but I didn't plan to snorkel at the port, so what did I care? What I ended up seeing of the rest of the island more than made up for the port's industrial feel.

And even though the day started and ended being overcast and cloudy it cleared up just before we left on our tour, so I took that as a good omen for what was to come.

***

Our group piled into two mini vans and drove the ten minutes or so to the tour company's office, where we were outfitted with snorkels, masks, fins and wet suits.

There were eleven of us from the ship and we varied A LOT in size, so it was amazing to see Paul, one of our guides, choose our wetsuits without asking anyone about our weight or our sizes, and not one single person had to try on more than one suit!

I'm sure experience was the key here; Paul had probably outfitted so many snorkelers in his career that this skill came naturally to him, and it's not as if he had to be concerned about color or style–have you ever seen anyone in a wet suit that is photo-worthy? (Although we did take photos.)

Once we were all outfitted, we piled back into the vans and drove to the beach.

Paul was the driver of our van and he was a veritable one-man comedy show; keeping us entertained and making us laugh the entire trip.

He was extremely good at imitating sound effects–barking dogs, police sirens, ambulance sirens, screaming tires, honking horns–so we never knew if our van was really screeching its tires as we rounded a sharp corner or if it was just Paul having fun with us.

He amused me, and I felt duty-bound to try to amuse him as well, so I began to add my own warped comments here and there throughout the drive, to see if he chuckled.

He did, while my sister-in-law rolled her eyes (maybe because this was day eight of our trip together and by now she pretty-much knew what was going to be coming out of my mouth whenever I opened it). But my goal here was to entertain Paul and the other passengers who didn't know me, and I did succeed with that…even Paul's colleague, a lovely young woman who sat in the front of the van with him commented that I should join him as a sidekick.

Finally (none too soon for Faye, I think), we arrived at the beach and headed to the water.

This is when I really began to get nervous.

What if I sink to the bottom like a rock? What if I float away to the open sea, never to be seen or heard from again? What if my mask leaks? What if my flippers flop? What if my wet suit attracts sharks? What if I look like an idiot?

But there was no stopping us at this point—we arrived as a group, we were heading into the water as a group, and fingers crossed we would all come back out of the water as a group.

Our guides were excellent—I can't say enough great things about them.

They watched over us, dragged some of us around on a surfboard-kind-of-thingy, offered assistance as needed, found fish and sea turtles and octopuses (really, it is octopuses—I looked it up), for us to look at under water, and continually counted heads to make sure that nobody did in fact float out to open sea never to be seen or heard from again.

And do you know what I discovered? I discovered that I LOVED snorkeling! I absolutely loved it!

Imagine my surprise!

Once I realized that I wouldn't sink to the bottom, that the wetsuit would indeed keep me bobbing around the surface like a rubber ducky in a bathtub full of water, I was more than happy to let go of the surfboard lifeline and explore the underwater sights around me.

Mind you, I'm not completely crazy–I made sure that I had fins and wetsuits in my vision at all times, and I made my way back to the security of the surfboard once or twice just to hold on, take a few deep breaths and enjoy the overall experience.

I loved every minute of the hour that we were in the water, and I would gladly have stayed longer, but it was time to swim back to shore.

Getting out of the water was even more difficult than getting in was –the wetsuit that was my friend and worked so well to keep me from drowning now became my foe– when I swam into shallow water and then reached down to try to remove my fins, waves caught me and pushed me onto my back, where I was buffeted about like a giant blue and black bottle that someone had carelessly tossed into the ocean.

Each wave sent me further toward the shore, so that was a good thing, but I knew that if I got too close to shore, in really shallow water, I wouldn't be able to stand up by myself because of my 'wonky' knee problems.

And that's exactly what happened.

There I sat, in the sand, holding my flippers in one hand and trying to keep myself glued to one spot with my other hand; I didn't want to be washed up onto the shore completely, to lie there like seaweed beached from a summer storm.

Finally, one of our guides spied me and came to my assistance. She dug her heels into the sand, held out her arms and ~~like a farmer hoisting a bale of hay~~ pulled me to my feet. Our little group trooped back to the vans, removed our wetsuits and toweled off and then enjoyed a quick snack before piling back into the vans to head back to our ship. I had lost my snorkeling virginity and I am happy to report that it was painless.

In fact, snorkeling on the Garden Isle of Kauai was probably the highlight of my entire Hawaiian cruise.

I thoroughly recommend it if you ever have the opportunity to snorkel there and I would be happy to provide you with the name of the tour company we used, as they were an excellent group of people.

Shortly after my snorkeling adventure I bought a mask and snorkel for me and this summer I plan to buy fins and a wetsuit, too.

Would anyone like to snorkel with me at my beach on the Atlantic coast? In all the years I've had a cottage there I've never laid eyes on a shark—only the occasional jellyfish and many little tickle-fish, so we should be safe as long as we don't float out to the open sea.

Hmm—maybe I should contact Paul to see if he'd be available as my snorkeling buddy; I'd certainly feel safe with him around.

And it's surely just a coincidence that as well as being comical Paul is also rather cute in a sun-browned, wind-blown, surfer-dude way?

Excuse me now while I look up his number...

"Hello, Paul?"

MY SEVEN AND A HALF MINUTES OF FAME

In one of my recent posts I wrote about my snorkeling adventure in Hawaii and how it was probably my top favorite activity while visiting the islands. And it was.

But I had one other top favorite activity on the cruise that took place on board the ship itself.

What was it, you ask? Well--my top favorite activity on board the ship was playing ukulele with a group of other like-minded cruisers!

Before we left on the cruise, Faye and I discussed whether or not we should take our own ukuleles with us, as we had read that there would be a ukulele lesson offered during the voyage.

But in the end we decided that we had enough luggage to worry about without adding musical instruments and cases to the mix, and we left them home (mine on the east coast of Canada and Faye's in Alberta, Canada).

We figured it wouldn't be worth the effort to drag the instruments along for just one ukulele lesson, and we knew the instructor would have instruments for students to play, so we cruised *sans* our really, really nice-sounding ukuleles.

That was a stupid decision on our parts.

While we waited to board the ship at the cruise terminal in Los Angeles we lined up ahead of a couple who were both carrying ukuleles.

Immediately a red flag began waving in my brain.

Oh, oh–what do they know that we don't know?

We started a conversation with them–were they perhaps cruise performers who were in the wrong line up?

Nope–they were a lovely couple of travelers from Utah– Steve and Shelley, and they were carrying their ukuleles with them because they liked the sound of these instruments, and they wanted to be sure they got the most out of the ukulele *lessons* they planned to sign up for on the ship.

Lessons--the plural of lesson? As in *'more than one'*?

Yep. Lessons. Definitely more than one, maybe as many as five or six.

The red flag in my brain waved more frantically.

Stupid, stupid, stupid...I told you to pack your ukulele but would you listen to me, your red flag? No, you ignored me and made the wrong decision...again. Will you never learn?

Apparently.

Once Faye and I boarded the ship and had an opportunity to peruse the list of activities that would be offered during our days at sea (four days going to Hawaii and four days returning from Hawaii), we discovered there were indeed ukulele lessons offered during most of those sea days. All we had to do was show up; everything else would be provided for us.

There were two sessions scheduled initially--one in the morning and one in the afternoon. Faye and I, being the geeky keeners that we are, decided to attend the morning session to get a head-start on our path to ukulele proficiency and eventual musical fame.

The lesson was scheduled to begin at eleven AM, so we figured if we waltzed into the room at ten-thirty we'd not only have our choice of the best seats in the lounge but probably even the best ukuleles, too.

It didn't work out that way.

At ten thirty the lounge where the lessons were going to be held was packed—who knew there would be so many other geeky keeners on board the ship with us?

We couldn't find a good seat so we decided to eat again instead (it had been an hour and a half since our last meal and lunch was still sixty minutes away), and we'd return to the lounge for the afternoon session, scheduled for two PM.

***

This time we were two of the first keeners to show up, and we plunked ourselves into comfy armchairs to wait for the instructor to arrive and perform his magic.

I'd never been a participant in group lessons before and wasn't sure I'd like receiving instructions that way, but I did.

For one thing, there was no pressure on me this way—I was simply one of about fifty people plucking away at ukulele strings, trying to make musical sounds come out of this tiny instrument.

For another thing, even if I was one of the pluckers hitting the wrong strings at times, the instructor was very experienced at teaching adults; he knew not to single anyone out in the group but instead made generalized comments and suggestions when he noticed one or more of us doing something incorrectly. We knew who we were and were able to modify our fingering or strumming accordingly, without feeling embarrassed by any extra attention.

And for the third thing, I at least had started playing a ukulele the summer before our cruise–some of the students had never even held a uke before, so I knew I probably wasn't the worst player in the group (or at least I hoped I wasn't).

Our first lesson was wonderful.

At the end of that lesson we had to sign up if we wanted to continue with lessons the next day; only people who signed up that day would be able to attend more classes.

Faye and I nearly bowled over a couple of elderly women on our mad rush to the sign-up sheet but luckily, other than a couple of bruised bums and one auburn wig gone slightly askew both women were okay.

After we added our names to the sheet we helped the women up and apologized to them, but also added that if they hadn't been standing between us and our musical dreams in the first place the mishap never would have happened.

I'm sure they understood.

***

We attended classes on six of our sea days, and on one of those days Faye and I went to two classes–the progressive beginner class number four in the morning and an afternoon intermediate class for players who thought they were ready for more intense ukulele instruction.

I knew I wasn't really ready, but Faye was going and I certainly didn't want to be left behind, so I gathered my courage and tagged along.

In the intermediate class our instructor showed us different strumming patterns and new chord progressions and a few other technical things—none of which I understood or would be able to recreate now, but I enjoyed the lesson anyway and did my best to keep up with the others.

In the progressive beginners classes I had no trouble keeping up.

Dave, our instructor, only asked that we all began together and ended together; he said that was all that really mattered in the long run.

And I think he was right about that--who cared if the middle part of the song sucked as long as the plunking sounds started in rhythm and ended in rhythm?

Dave always made a great show of signaling to us when it was time to stop playing—counting down—four, three, two, one, and STOP!

He'd wave his arms above his head and pump his fists in jubilation when we ended correctly, and when we didn't, he'd say, "Good try…now one more time…" and we'd do the song again and again until we did see the waving arms and the pumping fists.

During the first class he told us there was going to be a concert on the final evening of the cruise and said that all students were invited to take part.

Faye and I were excited.

After all, how many passengers on a cruise ship get the opportunity to entertain fellow passengers? Not too many, I think, other than karaoke singers or impromptu stand-up comedians in the bars.

But we had the chance to do this and we weren't going to miss out on it.

Fame and fortune here we come!

***

During each lesson we practiced our songs and built up our repertoire. We learned several chords, a couple of basic strumming techniques and how to smile while we played.

In the beginning, when we concentrated on strumming our ukuleles and placing our fingers just so on the frets, Dave told us that we looked as if we were all in the middle of writing a difficult exam.

He told us we had to at least **try** to look like we were enjoying ourselves, for his reputation's sake if nothing else.

"I have an image to maintain," he said, and "what would people think if my students all looked like they had guns to their heads at the concert"…so for Dave's sake, we learned to smile during our playing, even when we plunked a wrong chord.

We were like puppies wanting to please their master and get a pat on the head, or at least a fist pump in the air for good behavior.

Dave told us that we would play two songs at the final concert.

The first song, "Tiny Bubbles', would be ours alone--just the ~~incredibly talented~~ Ukulele Masters playing on stage for the adoring crowd.

Then we would play "Aloha Oe" while the ~~silly~~ talented Hula Dancers stood in front of us and performed their ~~stupid~~ graceful hula dance to the sounds of our beautiful music.

***

On the second-last day at sea we attended a dress rehearsal and found our spots on the stage. Luckily, Faye and I are on the shorter side of tall, so we got to stand on a platform one level above the ~~less-fortunate~~ taller ukulele players, who stood on the floor directly behind the ~~overly-dramatic~~ energetic hula dancers.

Faye and I could see and be seen and that was what mattered to us. We were going to get our fifteen minutes of fame that people talk about.

"All right, Mr. DeMille, I'm ready for my close-up."

On our final day at sea we relaxed and enjoyed another twelve or thirteen meals. We needed our strength to perform that night and everybody knows that food is fuel for the body, so we filled up our tanks.

Later that evening we took our borrowed ukuleles and our sheet music to the lounge where our talents would be showcased.

We were slated to entertain the audience at 'Who Wants to Be a Star' while the ballots were being tabulated to determine the contest winner.

So we knew we had a captive audience of at least every Pop Star performer's traveling buddies because they couldn't find out the contest results until we finished performing and left the stage, and I was determined I wasn't going to leave the stage until the audience clapped for us...clapped really hard and really long, too.

Soon it was time for us to take our places on stage. Faye and I positioned our bodies just so, to catch the best angle of light, and we turned on our smiles.

We were ready.

Dave lifted his arms and we struck the first few notes of "Tiny Bubbles" in unison, and we smiled and did our best to sing along with Dave while we played the chords.

I'm not sure how the middle of the song sounded, but we ended in unison and received a wonderful 'raised arms and pumped fists for our efforts.

Then it was the hula dancers turn. We played "Aloha Oe" while they performed, and even though they gyrated and wiggled around the stage I'm pretty certain all eyes in the audience were on the ukulele players, and more specifically, on Faye and me, and most specifically, on me.

I made sure I smiled as if I had just won the lottery...

Before I could say, "But I don't want to stop playing," it was time to stop playing.

The audience had the good sense to enthusiastically clap for us as soon as we finished our songs and we filed off the stage in an orderly fashion.

My fifteen minutes of fame ended up being more like a total of seven and a half minutes, so I'm thinking I have another seven and a half minutes of fame owed to me yet.

Faye and I celebrated our success with one last meal before we crawled into our beds for the night. The next morning we would dock in Los Angeles and fly back to Canada to resume our dreary normal lives.

Our ukulele-playing days on a cruise ship were over, probably forever.

But I'm going to keep looking for my next opportunity to experience the seven and a half minutes of fame still owed to me.

Any suggestions.

ALOHA HAWAII, HELLO ICE AND SNOW

It's official...my Hawaiian cruise is over and I'm back in the land of snow, cold temperatures, and ice. That's right, I'm back in Canada.

Today I have to travel from Alberta, where I've been visiting my brother Les and my sister-in-law Faye, to my home in New Brunswick, which means that I had to crawl out of bed at six o'clock this morning and be at the airport by seven in order to catch the first leg of my flight at eight. And I'll only arrive home late tonight, so it's going to be a long day, not helped by the fact that I didn't sleep last night.

I always find it difficult to sleep the night before I travel; I'm not sure why. Maybe I'm afraid of over-sleeping and missing my flight, or maybe I'm subconsciously nervous about traveling in general, or maybe it's just a coincidence because I have so many sleepless nights lately.

I don't know. All I do know is that sleep did not come to me last night, and I tossed and turned until my alarm sounded this morning.

Of course, not being in my own bed didn't help, either. Plus I've been sick.

On the cruise, Faye caught a cold and was kind enough to share it with me, and by the time we flew from Los Angeles to Vancouver to Edmonton, Alberta, I was completely filled up—lots of coughing, a stuffy head and nose, a fever, and generalized aches and pains.

All I really wanted to do was lie prone, but that was impossible to do while schlepping through cruise terminals and airports and security, and forget about it while on a plane—the seats recline approximately half an inch—I measured them to be sure, so you'll know I'm not exaggerating!

***

I spent the first couple of days in Alberta highly medicated and with barely enough strength to brush my teeth, never mind get dressed.

To sum it up, I would say that, until yesterday, I felt like "a great big bag of pig-poop".

But I still managed to enjoy my visit with Les and Faye We sat in front of the living room fireplace, surrounded by four dogs and three cats, and we watched movies and television shows that my brother had pre-recorded.

We also jammed together a few times—Faye played guitar and fiddle, Les played bass guitar, and I tried to strum the ukulele. It probably wasn't pretty but it was lots of fun!

We ate when we were hungry, drank when we were thirsty, and slept when we were tired.

Les wouldn't let us do any of the work in the kitchen--he said it was his job to prepare the meals and clean up afterwards, and he didn't want me in the kitchen with my germs. So Faye and I played games of Mario Kart and stayed out of his way.

Les not only prepared meals for us but twice a day he also put out food and water for the deer that wander into his yard in the cold weather.

He had fashioned serving trays out of large plastic garbage can lids that he screwed to saw-horses, and he filled these trays with rolled oats enriched with molasses.

The deer absolutely love his choice of food for them and they drop by several times a day to munch away on the buffet he provides.

After they eat the oats they move over to the drink stations—a birdbath and a blue bucket--complete with electric heating bands that Les attached to the containers to make sure the water doesn't freeze during Alberta's cold winter days.

This is no ordinary run-of-the-mill operation, and the deer seem to realize that.

They've told all their friends about it, I think, and if word-of-mouth keeps spreading through the forest they may have to form waiting lines at this buffet, just like cruise ship passengers, only probably more polite.

But I'm off track.

I survived my flights today without my sinuses bursting in my skull, and my son was waiting for me at the airport when my flight arrived.

We picked up a pizza on the way home, and after I eat, I'm heading to bed.

I plan to return to my normal routine of writing and blogging tomorrow, though, or the day after tomorrow, or whenever I feel like it. I'm funny like that; I don't like being predictable.

NO MORE BUCKET LISTS

Today I spent several hours online reading blogs about bucket lists.

I had no idea how important these lists are to people, of all ages, nor did I know that many of the items I'd see on these lists would be things that I have already done in my life.

And that got me to thinking, "Maybe when I'm feeling down and sorry-for-myself I should have a list of my own to read, a list that shows me some of what I've actually experienced and/or accomplished in the years I've been on this earth."

So that is what this blog post is about; it is a chronicle of items I would be able to cross off my bucket list if I had a bucket list.

Maybe once I make this list of completed items I'll start my own bucket list of things to do with the number one item on the bucket list being to make a list.

Here then, in no chronological order, are snippets of my life and my life adventures that I have experienced at some point in the past. Who knows what the future will bring?

1. Ride in a hot-air balloon. *I wrote about this in a previous post.*

2. Swim in the Atlantic Ocean. *I grew up swimming in the Atlantic Ocean so was used to turning a lovely shade of purple from the cold water.*

3. Carve my husband's and my initials into a rock. *I did this as a teenager when my future husband and I were dating, and I still have that heart-shaped rock in my jewelry box.*

4. Wade in the Pacific Ocean. *I don't remember if I actually swam, but for sure I at least went wading in the Pacific when I was visiting Vancouver Island.*

5. Stand on the most easterly point of land in North America. *This was Cape Spear, on the coast of Newfoundland, and I have pictures of me in front of the sign saying that it is the most easterly point of land in North America.*

6. See an iceberg. *When we lived in Newfoundland, Canada, I had the opportunity to watch many icebergs float by in the spring, and each one I saw was amazing. My husband had the chance to go out to one in a small boat and have a drink chilled with an iceberg ice-cube chipped off the berg right at that moment. He was awe-struck, too.*

7. Eat lunch on the banks of Loch Ness in Scotland and wait for Nessie, the Loch Ness Monster, to appear. *Alas, Nessie must have been having her afternoon nap at that time we were there, so we didn't see her. I'm sure*

I heard her snoring though, rhythmic peaceful sighs coming from deep in the lake.

8. Marry the love of my life. *I did marry the man of my dreams, and we remained happily married for over thirty-seven years before he died.*

9. Have children. *I have two amazing adult children whom I love more than anything, and luckily for me, they love me, too.*

10. Watch a meteor shower. *At our cottage we are privileged to be able to see the night sky so clearly, without city lights hampering the show of stars; this is where we see the best meteor showers and shooting stars.*

11. Watch the Changing of the Guards at Buckingham Palace in London, England. *My husband and I thought we should visit Queen Elizabeth while we were in London, but she wasn't home, so we stood outside her palace and watched the traditional changing of the guards. I guess if I ever decide to visit her again I should call ahead first to make sure she has the tea on, right?*

12. Fly in a single-engine plane. *I went flying with my brother as the pilot—it was fine, although I felt as if the wind really controlled us more than the engine did. I know I was wrong…I hope I was wrong.*

13. View the majesty of the Rocky Mountains from high atop The Whistlers, one of the Canadian Rockies most scenic and accessible mountains.

14. Ride in a Tram Car, also known as a Cable Car. *I have done this several times in Jasper National Park in Alberta, Canada—see # 13 above. Plus my daughter and I rode a cable car to the top of a mountain in St. Thomas, US Virgin Islands.*

15. Walk on a glacier. *I took a bus tour to the Athabasca Glacier, formed from snow that fell over four hundred years ago, at the Columbia Ice Fields.*

16. Take a cruise. *I've fallen in love with cruising and am going on my fourth cruise this fall.*

17. Go whale-watching on a ship. *Have done this a few times now—both in Nova Scotia and Newfoundland, and have had the joy of seeing whales each time.*

18. Spend a summer at a cottage. *I was lucky to be able to do this when my children were young, and now that I'm retired am slowly beginning to do it again. Cottage-summers are special, and I hope to take advantage of the summers I have left by enjoying simple cottage life during the warm months.*

19. Drive a truck. *Does my husband's Dodge Dakota count? I think it does.*

20. Drive a ride-on lawn mower. *Mastered that this summer at the cottage!*

21. Learn how to change an air filter in a push mower. *Ditto this summer at the cottage.*

22. Win money at a casino. *Last year a friend and I visited a casino and tried our luck at the slot machines. She put in*

$5 and promptly lost it; I put in $5 and won $60! I decided to quit while I was ahead and bought us both lunch!

23. Build a snowman. *I live in eastern Canada—I doubt there's ANYONE here that hasn't built a snowman at some point in life.*

24. Go camping in a tent. *Before we built our cottage my husband and I used to go camping, with a tent, sleeping bags and air mattresses. I never was a huge fan of camping, but we had no money and it was a cheap way to have a mini-vacation.*

25. Go ice skating. *Growing up, I skated on the swamp behind our home, on the pond down the road, and in our town's rink. Loved it but was never very good at it, although I really enjoyed skating around and around the rink with Gary holding my hand when we were teenagers.*

26. Ride a roller-coaster. *What can I say, I was a teenager and didn't know any better. You would never get me on one of those death-traps now!*

27. Make a quilt from scratch. *I think a lap-quilt counts for this, right?*

28. Milk a cow. *My parents kept one cow when I was a little girl, and I sometimes used to help my dad milk her. When my 'town' cousins came for a visit dad would ask them if they knew how to make cream, and when they said no, he told them they had to pump the cow's tail while he milked her, because pumping her tail turned the milk into cream. So my cousins would stand there and pump, pump, pump while my*

dad chuckled and encouraged them...'faster. pump faster.' My dad always had a strange sense of humor that I've inherited from him, I think.

29. Ride the Tube in London, England. *Did this with my husband in the mid 70s, back when the IRA was still leaving bombs around the city, and there were signs everywhere warning people not to touch packages left unattended or briefcases left on the Tube platforms.*

30. Sleep overnight on a train. *Have done this a few times in my life, twice trying to sleep in a chair in the 'coach' car, and twice when we traveled to and from Montreal, Canada with our two little children and had a cabin with bunk beds in it. I much preferred the cabin, by the way.*

31. Ride a double-decker bus. *Did this in London.*

32. Ride a bicycle. *Grew up riding—that's how we pretty much got from one place to another in the country. Rode my bike to my friends' houses and to school and to the store a mile from home. Loved my bike and the freedom it gave me.*

33. Climb a tree. *We had huge maple trees in our yard when I was growing up, and early on I learned how to climb my favorite one and perch on a board that a cousin nailed to a couple of branches way up high in the tree. I used to sit there for hours at a time, thinking my thoughts and watching the world go by. It was very peaceful; even now I sometimes have the desire (but not the ability) to climb a tall tree just to see if it feels the same way I remember it.*

34.   Get a massage. *Did this a few years ago because my kids gave me a gift certificate for one, but I didn't really much like it. I felt very exposed, with my 'back fat' hanging out and so I found it extremely difficult to relax. I just wanted to get it over with, more like a visit to the dentist than something that is supposed to help a person unwind and de-stress. I'm weird, I think.*

35.   Learn a musical instrument. *As I wrote about in a previous blog post, I'm learning to play the ukulele. I don't know if I'll ever become proficient at playing it, but I am enjoying the journey at trying to master chords and strumming.*

36.   Attend an art auction. *Cruise ships sponsor art auctions during sea days, and I attended my first one solely because they were offering free champagne. However I found that I enjoyed watching people with money (not me) bid on art pieces that I could never afford, so I went back to the auctions on my next cruise, too. Plus, did I mention they offered free champagne?*

37.   Own a business. *My husband and I owned a business called "Quality Creations" for a few years. Gary cut and sanded wood pieces and I painted them and sold them, plus I taught decorative painting classes and my students bought their wood supplies from us. This was in the nineties, when decorative painting/ tole-painting was at its peak.*

38.   Ride a horse. *A friend of mine owned horses and I had the chance to ride one when I was a teenager. I thought it was*

scary because it was HUGE, but the horse seemed gentle enough and thankfully I didn't fall off. I wasn't at all graceful getting on or off it, mind you, but I didn't fall, so I count that as a success.

39. Swim in the Caribbean Ocean. *Have done this several times now—always amazed at the color of the water.*

40. Visit the Tower of London. *Saw lots of crown jewels there—they looked VERY heavy—not sure how monarchs managed to wear them—must have had strong necks.*

I think it's time to stop now. I could add other items, such as feed chickens; play in a hay stack; visit a museum; attend live theatre; plant and weed a garden; watch the first landing on the moon on a black and white television; write poetry, short stories and essays and have them published; write a blog; make online blogging friends that I will likely never meet but that I feel close to anyway; and on and on and on.

What about you? Have you ever stopped to really think about what your life has been like up to now and about how you've spent your time?

Writing a 'completed' bucket list may be a good exercise for all of us to do every now and then, just so we can track the paths we've taken and think about all the good things, both large and small, that we've experienced along the way. We don't have to have climbed Mount Everest or walked the Great Wall of China to be able to say we did a lot of things in our lives that would perhaps be out of the ordinary for other people; all we have to do is think back to the times in our lives that were special in some way—those are the 'bucket list' moments.

I wonder what the future holds for me next?

ABOUT THE AUTHOR

Sylvia Morice writes fiction, creative non-fiction, essays, and poetry. Her work has been published in Canadian literary magazines, periodicals and newspapers. Her books are now available as eBooks via major online retailers and she has also published a paperback version of her award-winning short story collection Postcards From Home.

Connect with Sylvia Online:

Website: sylviamorice.com
Email: sylvia@sylviamorice.com
Twitter: twitter.com/sylviamorice
Blog: sylviamorice.wordpress.com
Facebook:sylvia morice

Sylvia Morice

Now That I'm Mature

Sylvia Morice